Tales From Ridgeway Furrow

Book 1
Save The Stream!

By

N.G.K

And

Sylva Fae

Tales From Ridgeway Furrow
Book 1 - Save The Stream!

By N.G.K. and Sylva Fae
Illustrations by Sylva Fae

Thanks to my friends Susie and Paul

Published by NGK Media 2020

First Printing, March 2020.

ISBN: 978-1-9160811-2-3

67489576KC

This book is part of the Harry The Happy Mouse series.

www.ngkmedia.com

www.harrythehappymouse.com

n.g.k. – To Isla, you make me smile every single day.

Sylva – To my three beautiful girls, Scarlett, Sienna and Sylva – your kindness and compassion for others is a constant inspiration.

Tales From Ridgeway Furrow

Book 1: Save The Stream!

Chapter 1

A Whistle and a Wander

"I must be the happiest mouse in the whole of Ridgeway Furrow!" said Harry as he looked out one beautiful morning.

The sun shone down over the little stone bridge, casting ripples of diamond light across the stream, which bounced onto the riverbank. The daisies and buttercups danced along to the music of the water on the gentle summer breeze. Harry took in the fresh air and smiled a twitchy nose smile.

"I do love my walks," said Harry. "When everyone else is asleep, the world is all mine."

Ridgeway Furrow truly was a magical place to live.

You see, Harry was at his happiest when he was helping others, and there was always someone in need if you went looking. Harry wondered if Mr. Frog needed a hand. Old Froggy was always getting stuck in the silliest of places. Harry often helped his friend down from high things a frog should not be hopping onto, but Froggy kept doing it and never seemed to learn!

Harry searched the bank and the stream for his friend, but instead of the familiar green face, something blue was bobbing along on the surface of the water. The little mouse leaned over for a closer look. It stood out because it was a very unusual colour against so many shades of green and brown.

"What is that?" Harry muttered to himself. "It doesn't look like an animal at all."

It seemed to be a plastic packet of some sort. The blue thing floated by and disappeared into the distance.

Harry continued to wander along. "Maybe I'll pick some blackberries for Katie," he thought to himself, starting to look around for signs of the lovely berries.

Harry's wife Katie made the best blackberry pie in the whole of Ridgeway Furrow. Harry's mouth watered at the thought of it.

"This is the perfect day for some blackberry pie," he thought. But before he could head out to the bramble patch on the edge of Sorrel Wood, he heard a cry.

"Harry, hey Harry! Can you help us please?"

The voice was muffled but it sounded just like Old Froggy. Sure enough, Mr. Frog hopped onto the path beside the mouse. He was carrying the blue plastic object in his mouth, the very same one that Harry had seen bobbing along minutes earlier. Mr. Frog tried to talk again, spat out the blue thing, and tried again.

"It's the water voles. They have a problem and they need our help," said Mr. Frog. He hopped about, eager to get going. "Come on Harry!"

"Of course," replied Harry, "Lead the way. But whatever is the matter?"

"It's their home. It's ruined, all clogged up with bits and things that people throw away. The children are trapped inside the burrow, and Vera Vole is so worried," Mr. Frog explained.

The two friends hopped and scurried to the water voles' burrow as quickly as they could. To Harry's surprise, the usually green leafy entrance was now covered in multicoloured packets and bottles and cans, and every few seconds another piece of rubbish joined what was already there. Harry scampered down the bank and found Vera Vole frantically trying to pull a bottle from her doorway.

"It's stuck, Harry! My children are inside. Oh, what am I going to do?"

"Don't worry, Vera. If we all help, we can soon clear up this mess."

Harry and Vera tugged at the bottle. It wouldn't budge.

"Try wiggling it!" suggested Mr. Frog, as he swam back and forth with the litter that had caught in the twigs along the water's edge.

Harry and Vera worked together, wiggling and tugging at the bottle until finally, it flew out with a 'pop!'

The little vole pups scurried out of the burrow and Vera hugged them to her. "Oh, I was so worried!" said Vera.

The pups didn't seem at all bothered and soon ran off to feast on the grasses along the bank where they chuckled and played together. They would have something to talk about at bedtime for sure!

"Thank you so much, kind mouse, and you too Froggy," said Vera with a smile, then she shook her head. "My home is clear for today, but I fear the litter will be just as bad tomorrow. You see, these twigs stop the soil around my burrow from being washed away in the stream, but they also catch anything that floats along. I love it here and I really don't want to move house. I'm just so tired clearing litter every day."

Harry and Mr. Frog said their goodbyes and set off for home. Harry was happy to have helped Vera Vole, but it seemed there was a bigger problem to solve, and this problem just wouldn't go away on its own.

Chapter 2

A Story to Tell

Harry left Mr. Frog and walked home with a heavy heart. Part of him was happy that he'd managed to free the vole pups, but knowing the litter would continue, made him sad too. He put on his happy face as he walked through the door and prepared for a cuddle attack.

"Daddy!" shouted his son and daughter, Alfie and Lizzie. They charged towards him, tails whirling and whiskers twitching. Harry opened his paws wide and the little ones jumped right in for possibly the biggest cuddle ever seen in Ridgeway Furrow, well, since Harry came home the day before at least.

"Hello, you two! Have you been good for Mummy?" asked Harry.

"Yes of course," squealed Lizzie, and told him all about how they had helped Mummy collect grass seeds for lunch.

"Hmmm," said Katie, "not so much helping...more like playing hide-and-seek in the long grasses and getting under my feet."

Alfie excitedly told how he was learning to fly with the butterflies. Harry giggled – a determined mouse can achieve almost anything, but flying probably wasn't one of them. "You know Alfie, if you think you can fly, then I'm sure one day you'll be able to," said Harry with a smile.

Harry smiled at his lovely family. He could just imagine how much fun they had racing around the big field. "You look tired Katie, my dear, why don't you sit down while I serve tea?" he suggested.

The mouse family tucked into a delicious meal of hazelnut roast with a leafy salad. Katie truly was a fabulous cook, but Harry always teased her that he was better. Soon, everyone sat back satisfied, with full tummies. Despite the lovely meal, Harry sighed. The events of the day were still troubling him.

"Daddy, Daddy will you tell us a story about your adventures?" asked little Alfie.

"I think Daddy is tired, Alfie. Why don't I do bedtime stories tonight?" suggested Katie.

"Oh, I think I can manage a quick story before I rest my paws," said Harry. "Now go get ready for bed, and don't forget to wash behind your ears...and Alfie, you still have crumbs stuck in your whiskers."

With the promise of a story, the little mice were ready for bed in the twitch of a whisker. Harry shuffled in between Lizzie and Alfie and snuggled them to him.

"Tonight, I'm going to tell you the story of how I rescued the baby voles. I was wandering down the stream, and all of a sudden, Mr. Frog came bounding along...."

"Did he get stuck on a log again?" asked Lizzie.

"Mr. Frog stuck on a log..." rhymed Alfie and giggled.

"No, not this time, Lizzie," Harry continued. "Mr. Frog took me downstream to Vera Vole's burrow. And do you know what I found there?"

"A giant cookie?" asked Alfie rubbing his tummy.

"A big scary fox?" said Lizzie, her eyes wide with fear.

"No, no. No cookies or scary foxes. I found the stream covered in litter. It had completely blocked the entrance to Vera Vole's burrow, and the babies were stuck inside!"

"Baby vole, stuck in a hole..." rhymed Alfie giggling again.

"Shhh Alfie," said Lizzie, poking her brother. "I want to hear the rest of the story."

"Well, Mr. Frog cleared all the litter from the stream. Back and forth he swam until every last bit was in a pile on the bank. But that wasn't the biggest problem, oh no! A plastic bottle was stuck in the entrance to the burrow. Vera and I tugged and tugged at the bottle until it flew out of the hole. The baby voles were rescued and we all went home for tea."

"Tell us another story, Daddy," both mice pleaded.

"No, I think that's enough for tonight. Now snuggle down and sweet dreams, my little ones." Harry tucked Lizzie and Alfie in and rubbed noses with each of them.

Harry wandered back to the living room and made himself and Katie a cup of nettle tea. He then slumped down in his favourite chair and handed Katie her cup as she sat down next to him.

"Now, why don't you tell me what's troubling you, my love?" she said kindly. "I heard the tale of rescuing Vera's pups, but that's not the whole story is it?"

Harry took a sip of tea and smiled at Katie. "How did you get to be so wise? You're right, it isn't the whole story. We cleared the litter today but Vera told me it's like that every day. Where is all this litter coming from? I saw two more bottles and a crisp packet floating by as I walked home. Poor Vera is at her wit's end."

Katie pondered for a moment as she sipped her tea. "I think we need to gather everyone together and clean up our stream."

"You're right, my dear," said Harry. "It's not fair that Vera should have to live like that. It looks a mess and it's dangerous for all the water animals. Can you imagine if one of Mr. Frog's froglets got stuck in a bottle...or a plastic bag got wrapped around a pup…? It's too scary to think about. But do you think the other creatures will help me clear up litter?"

"Of course they will," Katie reassured him. "You spend your days helping others, they'll only be too happy to repay the favour. Now let's get an early night because we have a big task ahead of us tomorrow."

"You're right my dear. On my own I can't do much, but all together we can do anything! That's my motto!" said Harry proudly.

"That's one of your many mottos dear."
smiled Katie.

Chapter 3

Gathering the Helpers

Early the next morning, Harry set off to round up as many helpers as possible. It was another beautiful day in Ridgeway Furrow and the countryside was full with singing birds, dancing butterflies and buzzing bees. It was a strange day for the happy mouse though. Usually, he was the one doing the helping, but today his mission was to ask for help from anyone he could find. He was sure his friends would join in once he explained the problem.

First stop, Mr. Frog's stone. Now, it might not seem like a very pleasant home, but Mr. Frog loved his muddy home under a pile of stones. He lived right on the edge of the stream, not far from Harry's home under the little stone bridge.

"Of course, I'll help you, Harry," said Frog when Harry explained the plan. "I'll swim downstream and round up all the water animals."

"Great idea," said Harry. "We'll meet up under the bridge."

Harry left the stream and headed uphill. The rabbits lived under the hedge leading to the big field. Harry often chatted with Flora Rabbit when he picked blackberries. You see, as much as Harry liked helping others, he also liked chatting too. Everyone in Ridgeway Furrow knew Harry.

The hedge had the best blackberry patch in the area and there was always plenty to share. He usually picked a few for the rabbits as well, before taking his home. You see, being a small mouse, he could sneak around the bramble thorns to get the juiciest blackberries where the other animals couldn't reach.

Harry found Flora stretched out, snoozing in a sunny patch of grass. Her kits, Clover, Daisy and Yarrow were playing nearby. Harry's children loved playing with the young rabbits. He really hoped Flora would agree to help, as Alfie and Lizzie would be so pleased to see their friends.

Gently, he woke the snoozing bunny. "So sorry to disturb you, Miss Flora. I was wondering if you could help me out today?"

Flora stretched, and yawned, "It's time I was awake anyway. What can I do to help, Harry?"

Harry explained the situation, while Flora listened, her eyes wide with worry.

"Of course, we'll help! We all drink down at the stream. Who knows what else is going into the water! What if it's not safe to drink any more...?"

Harry hadn't thought of that but she was right. It was an even bigger problem than he first thought. Flora promised to gather the other rabbits and meet down at the bridge.

Harry smiled to himself as he set off towards Sorrel Wood. He already had lots of helpers, and he still hadn't asked any of the woodland creatures. Of course, he whistled as he wandered. This was going to be a good day after all, and Harry knew that if they worked as a team, they could do anything.

The little mouse had just reached the jungle of ferns that marked the edge of Sorrel Wood when something big and black swooped down before him. Harry squealed and jumped back in fear. He looked around for somewhere to hide...

"What you doin' little mouse?" a croaky voice called.

Harry looked up at the big, black bird. His head was cocked to one side and his shiny eyes were full of fun and mischief. He didn't look too scary after all.

"Who are you?" Harry asked, then remembered his manners. "I'm Harry, pleased to meet you."

"The name's Jerry, Jerry Jackdaw. I was flying over and I thought I saw a wriggly worm. Mmmm, worms make a scrummy lunch...but it was just your tail," he said sadly. "Don't think I'm a fussy eater, but I'm not too keen on mouse tails".

Harry coiled his tail tightly around his legs. He didn't fancy it becoming a jackdaw's lunch.

"Well, that's a good thing!" said Harry

"So, what you doin' ?" Jerry tried again.

"I'm off to the wood to see if any of the animals...and birds," Harry added swiftly so as not to hurt Jerry's feelings, "would be willing to clean up the stream with me?"

"Clean up? Will there be shiny things. I love shiny things." Jerry hopped up and down in excitement.

"Err, yes there might be...perhaps shiny paper, or maybe shiny packets..." Harry replied.

"I'll help, I'll help. Show me where the shiny things are!"

Harry giggled at the bird's enthusiasm. It gave him an idea. It wasn't just jackdaws that liked shiny things, crows and other birds did too. "Jerry, would you be able to gather more birds and send them down to the little bridge? It would save me a job, and I still need to find the squirrels."

"Of course, of course! I can fly fast. I can get all the birds, and the squirrels too," Jerry replied. He puffed out his chest feathers, clearly pleased to be able to help. "But the first shiny things are mine – OK?"

"OK," Harry agreed, giggling. "You can have the first pick of all the shiny things we find."

With Jerry agreeing to round up the birds and squirrels, Harry set off back to the stream. As he passed under the old oak tree, he thought about asking Mr. Bat. He was sure Sebastian and his wife Darcy would help, but the trouble was that bats slept during the day. Harry wasn't sure how much help they could be anyway. He was just pondering the usefulness of bats when he hopped through the grass verge on the bank of the stream.

Harry couldn't believe his eyes! The bank from Mr. Frog's house, right down to the little bridge was filled with creatures. Squirrels scampered, rabbits hopped, and frogs and voles swam to the bank. Above, Jerry lead a mixed flock of jackdaws, crows, wood pigeons, and even a few sparrows. The birds landed on the top of the little bridge. The sound of excited chatter was in the air!

"See Harry, I told you they would help if you asked them," said Katie with a smile, as she got everyone into an orderly manner.

Harry smiled back at his wife, stood tall and prepared himself to help to organise the stream clean-up.

Chapter 4

Saving the Stream

Harry shouted as loud as he could:
"Thank you all for coming..." but his
voice was barely heard above the noise.
With chatter from a hundred woodland
creatures - squeaks, cheeps, squawks,
ribbits - the little mouse feared he
would never be heard.

"Ahem, would you like a little help
there Harry?"

Harry turned to see a giant hare
towering above him, his long whiskers

twitching. Sir Albert Hare was the mayor of Ridgeway Furrow. "Wow!" thought Harry, "even the mayor is here to help."

Sir Albert was the smartest hare you could ever imagine. He also towered above all of the other animals and had a booming voice that demanded respect.

"Yes please, Sir. A little help to get their attention would be appreciated."

Sir Albert raised his back foot and thumped the ground. It sent a wave of vibrations through the earth. As one, the animals and birds fell silent. They turned to look who had called for their attention.

The giant hare looked over the crowd, "Your attention please, fair creatures of Ridgeway Furrow. I am your Mayor!" His voice boomed out and every bird and animal listened. Even the little ones stopped tussling to see what was happening. "Katie and her husband Harry here have something to say. These tiny mice deserve our total respect and thanks, Ok, over to you!"

Harry cleared his throat, "Thank you all so much for coming to help. For safety, my wife Katie and I will take the youngsters to play in the field, we'll all be able to see them from where we are, and we'll all take it in turns to watch them."

A rabbit dad, a couple of squirrels and Dave the rat volunteered to help. Sir Albert raised a paw for silence and nodded to Harry to continue.

"Swimmers, your task is to collect the rubbish from the water and bring it to the bank. Land animals, please collect the litter from along the bank and pile it up here where it can't roll back into the water. And birds, I have a special task for you. I remember from when I lived in the city, that people have bins at the side of the road. I need you to take the rubbish and drop it in the bins. Now spread out along the stream, and let's work together to make our home a cleaner place for all who live here."

Harry threw both arms in the air and a cheer went up from the crowd below, and Harry beamed a wide twitchy-nose smile.

"You heard the mouse," said Vera, "We have a stream to clear. Let's get to work!"

Sir Albert turned to Harry, "Good work, young mouse, good work."

Katie smiled at Vera, "I'm so sorry to hear about what happened yesterday, it must have been so scary!"

"It really was," said Vera "I'm so grateful to everyone for helping today!"

"It's our pleasure Vera, you would do the same for us!" said Katie, putting her arm around her friend.

Good Old Froggy took charge of the swimming clear-up crew. They pulled packets from twigs, rooted out bottles stuck in the mud, grabbed cartons caught in roots, and took them to the bank. Working in pairs, they spread themselves out along the stream and gradually moved along until every patch of water was clear from below Vera Vole's home to beyond Harry's little stone bridge.

Up on the bank, Harry split the squirrels, rats, and rabbits into five groups. Each group formed a line up from the stream's edge. They passed the litter up the line, and the last animal in each group piled up the litter. Even Sir Albert joined in!

Jerry Jackdaw took pride in organising the birds to fly the litter to the bins, he wasn't very often allowed to be in charge of anything. Harry suspected the real reason was so Jerry could get the first pick of the shiny things for his collection.

After a couple of hours of hard work, the childcare team and the children returned with armfuls of blackberries to feed the workers. By the look of the red-stained paws and snouts of the little ones, they'd already eaten plenty of the delicious berries themselves.

After they'd eaten, Sir Albert offered to take care of the pups and kits, probably because he wanted a sit down after his hard work. Although he quickly found that he was also hard at work looking after the children! Harry wanted to personally thank each creature for giving up their time. He could see that everyone he thanked really liked the fact that he had taken the time to do it, and anything that encouraged the others was worth doing.

Soon, the stream and the bank were clear. All that was left was a pile of Jerry's favourite shiny things. He bundled the shiny packets; ring pulls and silver foil together. After thanking Harry for his shiny treasure, he flew off back to his home in the village.

"See you soon Jerry!" shouted Harry as he waved goodbye to his new friend. Harry liked Jerry. He watched as the bird's huge wings flapped slowly across the sky. "You know Katie," said Harry, "unexpected friendships are the best ones."

After thanks and goodbyes, Harry, Katie and the mice children went home. Harry hugged his family. It had been a great day to be part of the Ridgeway Furrow community, and Harry couldn't believe what they had done together.

"Oh I do love it when everyone pulls together," said Katie.

Harry nodded and put his arm around Katie as they walked along.

Chapter 5
A Little Girl

The next morning, Harry woke with a smile. The sun was shining down on him and he couldn't wait to get out for a walk.

"What a beautiful day!" he said, as he sat up and stretched out his arms with a big smile. He was not quite ready to open his eyes fully.

He chatted with Katie about his plans for the day - he wanted to check that they hadn't missed any litter, and pop back to see Vera Vole, just to make sure everything was OK. Katie kissed him goodbye and Harry picked up the lunch he had made the night before.

"I've made one for you too!" he said, as he waved goodbye.

Katie guessed he would be out for a while.

With a spring in his step, Harry set off. He marvelled at how beautiful the stream looked. The water sparkled in the sunshine, and every pebble shone like a precious jewel. Harry could see right to the bottom of the stream, and occasionally a fish would swim along. They nodded and Harry tipped his hat to them, even though he wasn't wearing one.

Harry reached the willow tree and decided to sit under its shady branches while he had a small snack. The wind rustled through the small leaves and the breeze was filled with bird song. He had just unwrapped his lunch when something bobbed past on the water. It looked like a plastic bottle - the same kind of bottle that had got stuck in Vera's burrow!

"Oh no, not more litter!" Harry cried. He dropped his packed lunch and scampered to the water's edge. The bottle was caught against a willow root, that stuck out from the bank. The little mouse leaned over to reach it....

"Danger! Danger!" squawked the familiar voice of Jerry Jackdaw. "Harry, quick! There's a little girl coming!" Jerry swooped down to warn Harry.

Harry turned to look just as a little girl ducked under the willow tree. He tried to scramble back down the bank, but he was leaning way too far over the stream. The mouse lost his footing and fell with a splash into the water.

Now, as you may know, mice can swim if they have to, but they really do prefer dry land to water. Harry splashed towards the bottle, thinking he could climb onto it, then jump onto the bank. There was still the problem of the little girl under the willow, but hopefully, he could sneak past without her noticing.

"Let's get back on dry land," he thought. "Then I'll think about the girl!"

That was the plan anyway, but as soon as Harry scrambled onto the bottle, it spun in the water. The movement freed the bottle from the tree roots and it set off on its journey down the stream. Harry dug his claws into the slippery plastic and held on. This was going to be a very bumpy ride.

"Little girl coming. Quick Harry!"
Jerry called, as he swooped over the
stream.

Harry looked up to see a huge hand
reaching out to grab him. He squealed
in terror and tried to back away but
there was nowhere to go, other than
into the water, and he really didn't
want to go back there.

"Poor little mouse. I'll rescue you," the
girl said. She grabbed the mouse and
bottle and lifted them out of the water.
"There you go, little mouse. You're safe
now."

The second the bottle touched the ground, Harry leaped and ran for the long grasses. His heart pounded but he'd survived. Jerry landed beside Harry and looked the soaking mouse up and down.

"You Ok my mousey friend?"

Harry nodded, shaking the water droplets from his fur. "I was so scared. When I lived in the city, people were mean and cruel. They kicked us, threw things at us or sent their cats to chase us away. This one cat, Lulu, chased me for over an hour once, they just don't give up! It sounds like a very cute name, but she really wasn't very nice to mice or birds for that matter." Harry shuddered at the memories and Jerry was now concerned at the mention of birds.

"I thought the girl was going to hurt me," said Harry. "I used to live on the streets, you know, it was hard!" said Harry.

"How did you get here?" asked Jerry.

"It's a long story, for another time," said Harry with a smile.

"Not all people are bad, you know," Jerry told him. "Some people leave food out for birds in their gardens. And shiny things...people always have lots of shiny things." The jackdaw's eyes twinkled with delight as he talked about all the special shiny things he'd found in gardens. Finally, after checking his friend was alright, Jerry said goodbye and took to the skies with a loud, 'caw!'

Harry was feeling better, and drier. He peeped out of the grasses where he'd been hiding. The little girl was still there. She was sitting in the grass, leaning up against the willow tree. The girl had a book in her lap and was mouthing the words as she read. She didn't seem at all scary now, and she had appeared to save Harry from the water. Maybe she was one of the nice people Jerry had been talking about.

Harry thought about what had happened. The girl hadn't been trying to hurt him, she'd been trying to help. Suddenly, Harry felt bad for running away. He really should say thank you - it was the polite thing to do after all.

Harry grabbed a hazelnut from the packed lunch wrapper and crept towards the girl. She looked up from her book and watched him creep towards her. Slowly, she reached out her hand and stopped just centimetres from his twitching nose.

"Hello, little mouse! Are you OK after your dunk in the stream?" said the girl.

Harry nodded. He could understand her words but he doubted she could understand mouse language.

The child giggled. "Can you understand me, little mouse?"

Harry nodded again and gave his best twitchy-nose smile. He inched forward and dropped the nut into her hand.

"Is this for me?" she said, delighted with her gift.

Harry nodded again. He wondered what stories she had in her book and crept forward to look. The girl stayed still, so Harry crept a little closer. To his dismay, the book was filled with black squiggles. Harry wished he could read people books. He had seen writing all over things, especially when he lived in the city, there were signs and numbers everywhere.

"Do you want me to read you a story, little mouse?"

Harry nodded once more and climbed up onto her knee.

"OK, this is a story about a fox who stole the moon...."

Harry listened in wonder, trying to remember all the words. It would make a fantastic bedtime story for Alfie and Lizzie.

As soon as the story was over. Harry climbed up onto the book and stood up on his hind legs to reach the girl. She leaned down to look at him. "Thank you for saving me and thank you for the amazing story." Harry knew she couldn't understand his words but she seemed to understand his actions.

"It's sometimes not what we say, but how we say it," said Harry.

Harry ran home with a smile on his face. It had been an amazing day and he couldn't wait to tell Katie and do bedtime stories with the children.

The children sometimes didn't believe Harry's tales, but this time, it would all be true.

Chapter 6

An Adventure

The following day, Harry promised to take Alfie and Lizzie for a picnic at the willow tree. The children couldn't believe that their father had met a real girl and made friends with her no less. They'd begged Harry to take them to meet her.

It was a beautiful day for a family outing. Harry loved his lonely whistle-wanders, but today, he would enjoy having Katie and his children by his side as they set off down the stream.

"There's nothing better than a family activity!" Harry said.

Alfie ran off ahead, wanting to be the first to find the girl. Katie called him back and thought she should sit the little ones down for a quick chat. "Look, I know you are very excited, but you need to be careful. Let Daddy go first. You see, not all people are friendly. If you run up to one of the bad ones, it could be very dangerous, and we wouldn't want anything bad to happen to you, sweetie."

"Your Mummy's right, my two little ones. I was very careful and watched and waited for a long time before I approached the girl yesterday. You must treat all strangers with caution, whether they are animal, bird or person," said Harry using his serious dad voice.

"Any stranger could equal danger," Katie agreed.

"Stranger danger, stranger danger," rhymed Alfie giggling, but for all his bravado, he slipped his paw into Katie's and held her hand tightly. He knew when Daddy used THAT voice, he was serious.

Harry scampered on ahead and ducked under the leafy branches of the willow. The tree hung so low that the willow leaves brushed the tips of the long grass. Underneath, was a green, leafy cave of shade, that swayed with the morning breeze. It was the perfect spot for a picnic. Harry could see why the little girl had chosen this place to read her book.

Harry stopped, sniffed the air. "Can you ever imagine a more perfect place for a picnic?" he said.

The rest of the family smiled.

As he looked under the willow, Harry was both disappointed and confused. The little girl wasn't there, but Old Froggy was, and he was not happy.

Harry waved to Katie and the children that it was safe to come out, then turned to Mr. Frog. "Hey Froggy, what's the matter? You look so glum!"

"Look!" said Mr. Frog stepping aside to reveal a pile of litter.

"It's back! After all our hard work yesterday, it's back. I'd planned to go fishing, but I didn't plan on fishing bottles and packets out of the stream. We can't spend forever clearing out our lovely home. Because we did such a good job yesterday it's not as bad, but we can't go on like this Harry."

"Oh no!" said Harry, shaking his head in dismay. "I just don't know how to stop it."

Katie joined the pair who were still staring at the pile of litter and shaking their heads. "OK, we did well to tidy up all of the litter that was already there, but we need to find the source of the problem. The litter flows downstream, so we must go upstream until we find where it is coming from," she said.

"Katie Mouse, you are a genius!" said Old Froggy hopping up and down in excitement.

Lizzie and Alfie were disappointed they couldn't meet the little girl, but they were soon in good spirits again. Harry and Katie explained the new plan - they were going on an adventure upstream. Lizzie and Alfie would be explorers!

So, Harry, Katie, the children, and Old
Froggy set off.

Harry nipped back into the house as they reached the little bridge, and came out with a pack full of food. He handed a hazelnut to each of the little ones to munch on as they walked. They would still have their picnic, but they would have a walk with a purpose too.

Harry gave Alfie and Lizzie a challenge to keep them occupied as they walked - Alfie was to spot bottles, and Lizzie was to spot packets. The little ones immediately took up the challenge and scampered on ahead. It gave Harry a moment to chat with Katie and Mr Frog. "What will we do when we find the source of the litter problem? It comes from people and two mice and a frog are no match for those giant people."

Mr. Frog nodded, and Katie patted her husband on the shoulder, "Don't worry about things we know nothing about. When we find the source of the problem, we will discuss what we'll do. If we need to, we will call a meeting for all the Ridgeway Furrow creatures. I have faith that we can sort this problem once and for all. Just remember Harry, no amount of worrying ever solved anything."

"As ever, you are right my dear," agreed Harry. "Let's just enjoy this walk for now."

It was a glorious day for a walk. The sun lazily peeped from behind candyfloss clouds, warming their backs as they walked. The familiar territory of Ridgeway Furrow, gave way to unfamiliar ground as the stream wound its way towards the village. The trees on the edge grew sparser, giving the explorers a clear view of the village beyond. The light hit the red and grey roofs of the buildings in the village. At the far side of the field, grey stone cottages dotted across the horizon, and the mice could hear rumbles in the distance. Harry explained to Mr. Frog that they were cars - noisy things that growled and transported people from one place to another.

"The road's one place that no animal in Ridgeway Furrow should ever visit," said Harry.

Froggy and Katie knew that Harry was thinking back to his time in the town, and they weren't surprised to see a small tear in the corner of Harry's eye. None of the animals wanted to ask Harry why he was sad, they didn't want to upset him even more, but Harry had obviously had bad experiences with roads.

Alfie and Lizzie came running back breaking into the silence. "Quick! We've found it! We found the litter!" Alfie shouted excitedly.

"I was counting packets but there were way too many to count. There's a mountain of litter...and strangers." Lizzie added, her eyes wide with worry.

"Strangers?" said Harry. "Right, you lot stay here, I'll creep ahead to check it out."

Chapter 7

Naughty Children

Harry crept forward, keeping close to the grass verge which hung over the bank of the stream. He could hear voices of people ahead and loud splashes as if something had just dropped into the water. He climbed the verge and jumped up onto a log for a better look.

There they were! The source of the problem - three little boys. Harry watched as they pushed and shoved one another. The biggest of the three grabbed a bottle and threw it as far as he could. It landed with a splash and bobbed down the stream towards Ridgeway Furrow. But that wasn't the worst of it. Harry looked around in horror at the mess and destruction.

Along that edge of the stream was a wire-mesh fence, it ran far into the distance, as far as Harry could see. These fences were never a problem for the mice, as they could easily fit through the gaps, and usually, they kept the people out. Not this one though, this one had a child-sized hole ripped in it. It appeared that these children had made this place their den. Empty cans, crisp packets, bits of paper and plastic bottles littered the ground, hung from branches and blew into the stream. All along the wire mesh fence was a layer of litter, blown there by the wind. It collected at the bottom.

Harry shook his head in dismay. Even if the animals cleared all the mess up, the children would be back to throw more into the stream. Harry hung his head and trudged back to tell Katie and Mr. Frog. Maybe Katie would have a plan.

As he rounded the bend, Harry was surprised to find his family and friend gone. Harry glanced around, confused and extremely worried. Where could they be? Then he saw the reason - sitting further up the bank was the little girl from yesterday.

"Katie, Froggy!" he called, "You can come out. It's OK, it's the kind child from yesterday."

"Oh Harry, we were so worried," Katie called out from under a tree root. "When you didn't come back, we thought the people had captured you."

"Oh I'm fine, but unfortunately the situation is rather worse than I thought." The little mouse explained to Katie and Mr. Frog what he had found.

Katie listened, and thought…" I wonder if your new friend can help? We are too small to take on three children, but maybe another child could?"

Harry crept towards the little girl. Like yesterday, she sat under a tree reading a storybook. Harry tapped on her toe and waited. The girl looked up from her book, then squealed with delight. It made Harry jump, but he quickly realised that the girl was excited to see him.

"Little mouse, you came back! I've been hoping you would! Do you want me to read you another story?"

Harry called for the others to join him. The girl looked in amazement as three more mice and a frog hopped up the bank and sat beside her.

"Oh, I have got quite an audience today!" said the girl, making it obvious that she wasn't going to hurt them in any way.

"OK, this story is about a young wizard called Harry, who goes off to a magic school..." the child stopped reading to look at the mouse, who was jumping up and down in excitement and pointing at the book. "Do you like this story?" she said.

The mouse shook his head, pointed to himself, then to the book again. The girl scrunched up her forehead, puzzled. Then it hit her - "Harry! Is your name Harry too?"

The little mouse nodded and squeaked, and the others joined in. "Well, I guess I should call you Harry then. My name is Isla. Pleased to meet you all." The girl gave out a wonderful smile that made all of the animals feel relaxed.

"Wow Harry, that's amazing!" said Katie. "I never thought a little girl would be able to understand us but we may just be able to talk with this one!"

Chapter 8

Help from the Little Girl

"We need to get the child to follow us. Maybe if she sees the litter, she will help?" Harry said to Katie and Mr Frog.

"It's certainly worth a try," agreed Frog. "I'll go grab some litter out of the stream. Harry, Katie - you try to bring the girl." Froggy hopped off and landed with a splash in the stream.

Isla clapped her hands and giggled. She put her book down and crawled to the water's edge to watch Mr. Frog who was now swimming through the clear water.

"What are you doing little frog?" she pondered out loud as she watched him dive under the shallow water, and emerge with a plastic bag in his mouth. He swam to the edge, and the mice took the bag from him and placed it on the bank. The frog swam to the opposite side, grabbed a plastic bottle and pushed it to Harry's paws.

"Oh, I see. Yesterday when I rescued you from the stream, you were trying to clear the litter. Is that right, Harry?" Isla asked.

Harry and Katie nodded. "I think this plan may actually work, Katie!" Harry said with glee. "Now we just need to get her to follow us upstream, to where the naughty children are."

Harry tapped on Isla's hand and ran a few steps. Then he turned around and waited. Isla just watched him. Harry tried again, and Katie nudged the girl with her nose.

"Oh, you want me to follow you, Harry? Is that it?" Isla said.

She wasn't sure but she was convinced these creatures were trying to tell her something. She wished she could understand what they were saying to her, but she knew they were doing a pretty good job anyway.

Harry nodded in response and scampered on a little further. Isla stood up and then followed Harry and Mr Frog. Katie decided to stay back with the little ones as they were happily playing - jumping on and off Isla's book. The plan was working so far, Harry just hoped that Isla would understand the problem once they got to the den of litter.

As they walked up the stream, Isla couldn't stop talking, telling Harry about the cottage she lived in with her mum, dad, and big brother, Archie. From what Harry could tell, it was over the other side of Flora Rabbit's field - a short walk for a girl but a long trek for a mouse, maybe even a day or two. They arrived at the corner of the high wire fence.

"See that building over there, Harry?" Isla said, pointing to a large red brick building across a patch of grass. "That's my school - Willow Bank Primary, and that grass over there is our playground. See that tree - the big oak? That's where I sit at playtime to read my book, lots of other children sit there too, the ones that like to read anyway. Sometimes we run around and play too, but sometimes it's nice to take it easy and relax in the sun. Reading is my favourite thing in the whole world," Isla said with a smile.

"School has finished for the day now though. My mum lets me play out here providing I don't leave the field...."

Harry always wished he could read, he used to look at the pictures in the newspapers and magazines when he lived in the city. The animals around him always told each other stories, and sometimes a travelling animal would pass through and tell stories from far away.

Harry and Mr. Frog stopped. They had reached the bend just before the den where the children were throwing litter around. Isla stopped talking and listened. The voices of the three children carried through the trees, breaking through the beautiful countryside noises. Isla crept forward and peeped around the bend. Her eyes grew wide....

"Oh Harry," she whispered, "I can see what the problem is now. Those naughty boys have broken through the fence! Mr. Worrall, our headmaster, is going to be so angry when he finds out."

Harry nodded. He was so relieved she had understood. He shouted to Mr Frog that they should head back to Katie and the children and then beckoned to Isla. The three unlikely companions headed back and Harry quickly told Katie what had happened.

"Harry, I'm so sorry those boys have messed up your stream. I'm going to tell my mum and she will speak to Mr. Worrall tomorrow. Charlie, Zach, and Theo are going to be in so much trouble! They're such naughty boys, and bullies too!" Isla grabbed her book and got up. "I'll come to the willow tree after school tomorrow. Bye-bye little mice. Bye-bye frog." Isla turned and ran back across the field, towards her home.

Harry, Katie, Mr. Frog, and the children cheered. They had successfully completed their mission, found the source of the litter problem and Isla was going to help.

"But why do those boys do it Dad?" asked Alfie.

"Maybe they don't realise they're causing a problem for someone else, maybe they just think they're having fun," said Harry, always trying to see the good in everyone.

"But we still haven't had our picnic," Alfie whined, rubbing his tummy.

"Yeah Dad, you promised us a picnic by the stream!" Lizzie added.

Katie laughed, "OK, I think we all deserve some fun after our long trip." She opened the bag and got out the leaf wraps. The little mice squeaked with delight at all the delicious food. The mice dined on clover and sorrel salad, beechnut pie, followed by Katie's special carrot cake. Mr. Frog politely declined and hopped back into the stream to catch some flies – that was more his kind of thing after all.

"Oooooh, flies for tea! Yuk!" said Alfie, and pretended to be sick. Lizzie giggled.

"Alfie, that's rude," said Harry. "All animals like to eat different things. Mr. Frog didn't say 'Yuk!' when Mummy offered him a slice of carrot cake, now did he?"

Alfie shook his head, "I guess not. Can I have Mr. Frog's slice of cake then?"

Harry couldn't help but laugh at his young son's ability to think with his tummy. The family enjoyed a lovely afternoon together on the bank of the stream, the kind of day where they didn't do anything special, which meant that everything they did was special, because they were together.

The little mice played hide and seek in the long grasses, Mr. Frog found a cool flat stone to sunbathe on, and Harry and Katie lay back and relaxed in the sunshine. It had been another successful day.

"Another wonderful day that we won't forget in a hurry!" said Harry.

Chapter 9

The Ridgeway Furrow News
Network.

Harry couldn't wait to meet up with
Isla the following day. He remembered
she'd said something about meeting at
the willow tree after school, but he had
no idea when that would be. You see,
mice do not measure time on watches
and clocks as people do.

Time in Ridgeway Furrow is measured
by the shining of the sun, meal times
and whether or not it is raining. For

Harry, no rain meant a long stroll, mild rain meant a swift walk, and heavy rain told him it was time to stay indoors. Today was a long stroll day.

As he had no idea about time, Harry ran to the willow tree just after breakfast. Of course, Isla wasn't there. Harry pottered to the stream to look for litter but even that didn't take long, as there was not even a sliver of plastic floating in the water.

The mouse settled himself under the tree to wait, actually quite pleased he had some time to himself. Harry loved his family, but everyone needs to make time for themselves sometimes. It was another gloriously sunny day. Harry lay back in the grass and watched the sunbeams dancing between the branches. Way above, he saw the birds soaring across a cloudless sky. He watched mesmerised, as they dipped and dived, gliding on the breeze. Harry let out a big yawn.

"What a great day to be a mouse." he whispered.

He was still tired after the adventures of the day before. "Just a little snooze..." he started to think as his eyelids closed.

Harry dreamed of Ridgeway Furrow without litter, the beautiful stream, and all of the animals playing and laughing together as the sun went down on a summers' evening....

"Harry...Harry..." a distant voice called. Something sharp poked him in his tummy. "Harry...wake up, my mousey friend!"

Harry opened his eyes and blinked in the sunlight. The pokey thing was a long black beak, attached to a shiny, feathered head. Harry blinked again and looked into the mischievous eyes of Jerry Jackdaw.

"How can you sleep at a time like this?" laughed Jerry.

"Oh, you know," said Harry, "a little snooze never did anyone any harm".

"No time for snoozing. Tales to tell...things happening...exciting things..." Jerry babbled excitedly.

"What exciting things?" Harry was awake now and sat up to give Jerry his full attention, he didn't want to appear rude, and the Jackdaw was obviously excited.

"Upstream...I went to see...things are changing...lots of shouting...the shiny things are going," Jerry continued.

"What are you talking about?" Harry asked, puzzled.

"What he's trying to say in his birdbrained way, is the stream is being cleared, up by the school."

Harry turned to see Mole walking towards him. Mole settled down on the grass beside Harry.

"What are you doing here, Mole? Aren't you usually asleep at this time?" Harry asked. He wondered if he might still be dreaming.

"Hmmm, well I was trying to sleep but I was awoken by some animals walking loudly past my hole saying that the litter was gone!" Mole replied and winked.

"I just can't believe it!" said Harry.

"But how did they know about the litter situation?" As far as Harry knew, only Mr. Frog, Katie, and the children knew the events of yesterday.

"Well, Old Froggy told Vera. The voles told the squirrels...and you know what squirrels are like for passing on news! It didn't take long before one of the rat twins (I can never tell them apart) came to tell me and Martha," Mole replied.

"And I heard from a wood pigeon, who'd heard from a crow, who was listening in when Mrs. Squirrel told Flora Rabbit. So I flew off to look for myself," Jerry added.

Harry was just about to ask Jerry to explain what he'd seen when Isla poked her head under the willow branches.

Mole scurried up the bank and dived into a hole in the grass verge head first, which caused Harry to giggle. Mole hadn't been very brave at all, and the sight of a mole diving head first into what must have been a deep hole, looked very funny! Jerry fluttered to a branch and leaned down to listen.

"Hello, Harry!" Isla said when she saw the little mouse. "I was hoping you'd be here again." She sat down on the grass next to Harry. "I have so much to tell you!"

Harry listened in silence as Isla explained how her mum had spoken to the headmaster and he had gone down to the hole in the fence at breaktime and caught the three naughty boys red-handed. Harry didn't quite understand why having red hands was important but he was relieved the boys had been caught.

"Mr. Worrall made them clean up all the litter after school. They were not happy!" Isla clapped her hands in glee. "Then Mr. Hobbs, the caretaker, fixed the fence so they can't do it again."

Harry climbed up onto her hand and hugged her finger. He wasn't sure how to thank a child, but he hoped she would understand. He looked up into her eyes and gave her his best twitchy-nose smile. Isla smiled back but she looked sad too. The little mouse wished he could ask her what the matter was.

As if she'd read his mind, Isla sighed and started to talk to the little mouse. "Oh Harry, I'm glad I could help. At least one thing has gone right. I'm supposed to be taking photographs for the school photography competition but I've no idea what to do. You see, the theme is 'Happiness'. My brother, Archie is taking photos of his football team, my friend Scarlett is doing hers on her dance class, and Billy is taking pictures of cakes in his mum's bakery. What can I do? I'm happiest when I'm sat reading under this tree. It's hardly an exciting subject, is it?" She sighed again and gently set Harry down on the ground.

"I love taking photographs, but I'm not very good with ideas, and I love being out here in the country, but it's not great for the theme of 'Happiness' – just a load of trees and a stream. I've never won any of the competitions in school, I always have to sit there and watch other children go up and get their prize. Of course, I'm happy for them, but it is so disappointing. I would love to know how it feels to win something." Isla put her arms around her legs and put her head on her knees.

Harry had an idea! Isla had helped all the creatures by reporting the boys who'd messed up their stream. Maybe the animals could repay her kindness! He called to Jerry, who'd been listening in from above, "Hey, Jerry, do you think you can gather as many animals as possible and bring them here?"

"Sure thing, boss. I'm fast. I'm the fastest jackdaw in the whole of Ridgeway..." Jerry's words faded into the breeze as he'd already set off on his mission.

"Mole, are you still hiding down there?" Harry shouted down the bank.

A whiskered black nose poked out of a hole. "Come on out, Mole. This little girl is so kind. She won't hurt you."

Slowly, Mole crept forward towards Harry, keeping one eye on the girl, who was still sitting with her head on her knees. "You sure this is safe, Harry?" Mole asked, fearfully.

"Of course! This is Isla. She is the girl that stopped the litter from getting into the stream," Harry explained. "Can you gather Martha and any other animals you find along the way. I have an idea to thank Isla for her help."

"Caw! Caw! Meeting at the willow tree. Caw! Caw! Meeting now!"

Harry laughed as he heard the jackdaw soar overhead, summoning animals. Jerry was certainly proving to be a helpful friend to have. People had their little magic boxes that they talked into to pass on messages, but he had Jerry, and the noisy jackdaw was very efficient at getting the word out.

Chapter 10

Repaying the Kindness

First to join him were Katie and the children, followed by Mr. Frog and the froglets. Mole arrived shortly after with Martha. Martha Mole hung back shyly, a little in awe of the little girl. Next to the willow, came a tumble of fur that bounced and squeaked with excitement and Harry was nearly bowled over by the excited young kits.

"Sorry, Harry," said Flora as she tried to calm her little ones down.

Next, Sir Albert Hare strolled under the willow boughs, with as much authority and grace as a hare could possibly have, accompanied by his friend Mac Badger. Finally, Jerry appeared overhead, leading a rather mixed flock of birds - another jackdaw, two crows, a wood pigeon, and the kingfisher from the pond down the hill.

Yet again, Harry was astounded by the kindness of his friends, to come running when he asked for help.

Katie seemed to read his mind, "The creatures are happy to help you, my dear. You do have a reputation around

Ridgeway Furrow for helping any creature in need. You know how happy it makes you feel when you do a good deed? Well, now they get to feel happy doing a good deed too."

Harry smiled and nodded to his wife. He realised that some of the animals were staying as far away from Isla as possible. "My friends, this little girl is also a friend. She is the one who stopped the litter from going into our stream. She saved our stream! Now, she needs a favour from us. Do you see that black box in her hand? That is a camera, and people use them to take photographs...."

"What's a photograph?" Yarrow asked, creeping up to the camera and sniffing it.

"A photograph is a picture of whatever the camera is pointing at," Harry explained. (He had once chatted with a dog in the city, who complained that her owner was always dressing her up in frilly hats and taking photographs of her. The dog said it made her look silly but it made her owner happy.)

Harry looked at the little ones - they still looked confused. "Nevermind about the camera. What I need you to do is sit on a log, or a branch or in the stream, and stay very still while Isla points the camera at you - OK?"

"Will it hurt?" asked Clover, hiding behind Lizzie.

"Not one bit. You just keep still until the camera goes 'click'."

"It's extremely important that we look happy!" said Harry. "Which shouldn't be a problem for you lot!"

The assembled animals laughed and relaxed. All the animals nodded and agreed.

"I'll go first to show you how it's done," said Harry. He hopped onto Isla's chest and tickled her nose to get her attention.

Isla rubbed her nose and discovered the tickle was a little mouse. "Oh hi, Harry." Isla suddenly caught sight of the medley of birds and animals huddled under the willow. Harry nudged the camera and pointed to a log. He climbed up and sat, his tail curled perfectly in the air.

"Ooh, stay there, Harry. That would make a brilliant photograph." Isla grabbed the camera, fiddled with the buttons, then 'click', the picture was taken.

"See," said Harry, "That's it! Simple!"

Isla looked at the photographs she had taken on the screen of the camera, she could hardly contain her excitement, she had never seen such a good picture of a happy mouse. I'm going to call that one "Harry The Happy Mouse!" she said.

"I want a photograph..." Yarrow bounded to Isla and pointed at the camera, then hopped back to his sisters. The three young kits fluffed out their tails and pointed their ears high.

Isla giggled and clicked the camera once more. "I get it, Harry. I get it! You've brought your friends here so I can get some interesting photographs. Of course! It's not just reading here that makes me happy, it's being in this beautiful place surrounded by wildlife. This is amazing!"

Harry took charge, leading Isla to each of the animals in turn. Jerry posed proudly on a low branch so that Isla could take a close up of his rainbow-sheened feathers. Mr. Mole and Martha pretended they were just emerging from their hole – Isla snapped their velvet noses just peeping out. Sir Albert struck a noble pose up on the bank, looking out over the fields, and Mac Badger curled up pretending to be asleep in a patch of leaves.

Each of the animals and birds tried to make their picture better than the last with interesting poses, but Kingfisher stole the show. He flew high above the stream, then dove, as if to catch a fish. Just as he was about to hit the water, he slowed in mid-air, his turquoise wings fanned perfectly and his beak just skimming the surface of the stream.

"Wow!" said the animals and Isla in unison.

Kingfisher landed next to Katie and Harry. "I know what the people like!" he said. "For some reason, they seem to like taking photos of me. There was this one time when a man and a woman stayed in a little tent where I live, for days! Their camera lens was pointing out of the tent the whole time. In the end, I just felt sorry for them and flew past, they took lots of pictures then left!" said Kingfisher, very proud of himself.

Once all the pictures had been taken, Isla ran back to the shady spot under the willow. She fiddled with the camera once more, then beckoned to the animals to look. You would never have believed how shy Martha was just an hour before because she climbed right up onto Isla's knee to get the best view.

Isla slowly scrolled through the photographs she'd taken. She held the camera screen out to show each creature their picture.

"Look at me. Look at me! Do I look handsome? I do, don't I? I do look handsome," Jerry crowed and fluffed up his feathers in pride. "You may think people want pictures of you Mr. Kingfisher, but look at me!"

Isla couldn't understand the chatter between the animals but she watched their reactions to the pictures. She felt they must understand. It was far too much of a coincidence for all these wild creatures to show up just as she needed a subject for the photography competition. And for them to be so tame.

Then, Isla had an idea. "Harry, I want to take one last picture, but I need everyone all together. We need to stay very still until I say we can move. OK?"

Harry nodded. Isla shuffled the moles, bunnies and baby mice off her knee and placed the camera on a log. She knelt down to look through it, fiddled with the buttons, then sat back in her original spot.

"Quickly everyone, gather around me...."

The little ones leapt back onto Isla's knee, Jerry and the birds perched on her head and shoulders, Albert and Mac sat either side with Flora, Mr. Frog and the Moles snuggled in front. Isla held out her hand, and Katie and Harry hopped on. She held the mice up next to her face, just in time for the camera to go, 'click'.

Chapter 11

The Happiest Mouse in Ridgeway Furrow.

Several days went by. Several quiet days, in fact. Harry had enjoyed all the adventures he'd had with his friends, but he was quite relieved to go for a whistle and a wander without incident. Harry learned a bit about people time, and he soon realised that Isla came to the willow after dinner but before it was time to go back for supper.

Talking of supper, since he'd become the first creature of Ridgeway Furrow to make friends with a little girl, he'd become quite a star. Every animal wanted to invite Harry and the family for tea, so he could tell the tales of his adventures. Now, Harry was a modest mouse, but he did love telling a story!

Harry was just pottering back to the little bridge to meet up with Katie and the children when the silence was broken....

"Caw! Caw! Harry! I have news!" Jerry swooped, skidded and landed at Harry's paws.

Harry laughed at his excited friend. "Come back with me, I bet Katie will want to hear all about this."

Jerry could barely contain his excitement, but soon they were back at Harry's home under the bridge. "Caw, caw! Hurry, hurry. Tales to tell!" Jerry shouted through the doorway.

Katie hurried the little ones outside to see what all the commotion was.

"I think Jerry is going to burst if he has to wait any longer to tell his tale, Katie!" Harry laughed and turned to the jackdaw who was hopping from one foot to the other impatiently.

"I went to school...Isla's school...I went every day and peeped through the window. Jackdaws are good at peeping! They have this thing in the morning that they call 'assembly', they just all seem to sit in the hall while an adult tells a story! Today I saw the big person and the photographs were all hanging around the room and the children were stood in front of them...then I saw Isla. The big person gave Isla a shiny thing...the shiniest shiny thing ever and all the other people cheered. Isla won the photograph competition! She won!"

"Hurray!" shouted the mice.

"All of her friends were hugging her, and she was handed a big piece of paper with a huge '1st' on it! Then two other adults and a young boy all hugged Isla and lifted her in the air!"

"That must be her Mum, Dad, and Archie!" said Harry.

"But the best bit," said Jerry, very excited to finish his story, "Was just when she was about to leave, Isla looked out of the window and saw me, she waved and held up her shiny thing and piece of paper!"

"Wow! If we hurry back to the willow tree, we might see Isla before teatime," Harry suggested. The little mice didn't take much persuading and scampered off ahead. Harry and Katie sauntered behind, holding hands. "It couldn't have happened to a nicer little girl!"

"I'm so happy for Isla," Katie agreed. "She always wanted to win something!"

Harry and Katie were just about to duck under the willow branches when they heard squeals coming from beneath the tree.

"Daddy, Daddy, look!" Lizzie squealed.

"Caw! Caw! So handsome...look at me!" Jerry crowed in delight.

Harry looked up through the willow leaves to see his children and Jerry hopping around Isla's feet as she placed something next to the tree trunk. Isla stepped back to reveal the group photograph.

He scurried forward for a closer look. Katie sidled up next to him and put her paw in his. Together they gazed at the picture.

"Do you like it?" asked Isla.

"I won, everyone. I won!" shouted Isla, "and it's all thanks to you! I've never won anything like that before!"

The competition had been judged by a famous wildlife photographer, and he had told the children that he had never seen such clear pictures of animals, and certainly not a kingfisher.

"I imagine he loved the pictures of me too?" said Jerry, and everyone laughed.

Harry looked at each of the animals in the picture - Jerry, proudly stood upon Isla's head, his little ones beamed for the camera, and his and Katie's own smiles matched the one on Isla's face.

"This is for you," said Isla, handing over the photo of the group "Nothing would make me happier than to know this photograph will be displayed in Ridgeway Furrow.

Harry looked at his friends and family, then nuzzled Katie's nose with his own, and sighed a happy sigh.

Isla sat down with the animals and told them all at length about the competition, and all animals stayed to listen, sitting around as the light changed from yellow to orange, to dark red.

Once they had said goodbye to Isla and the light started to fade, they all walked back together, and as they passed their homes the group of animals got smaller and smaller. The moonlight lit the last few steps up to Katie and Harry's home, they each carried one of the children who were fast asleep. The light had faded over Ridgeway Furrow, and there was electricity in the air. Harry looked at the sleeping children, then looked at Katie and said: "I must be the happiest mouse in Ridgeway Furrow."

The End

CPSIA information can be obtained
at www.ICGtesting.com
Printed in the USA
LVHW041631140720
660690LV00010B/1607